Porch Night On Walnut Street

Porch Night

On Walnut Street

Alex Richardson

Plain View Press
P. O. 42255
Austin, TX 78704

plainviewpress.net
sb@plainviewpress.net
1-512-441-2452

Copyright Alex Richardson, 2007. All rights reserved.
ISBN: 978-1-891386-88-6
Library of Congress Control Number: 2007931094

Artwork provided by Z-knuckle and B-dawg.

Contents

Alphabed   11

    Paradise Off Main   13
    A Portrait Of Wanda   14
    Vacation   15
    Casino Hospital   16
    Changing Penelope's Diaper   17
    Another Reason I Am Not a Painter   18
    Self Portrait   19
    In a Booth At the House Of Pizza,
        Waiting On the Odysseus Platter   20
    Deciduous   21
    Nightshape   22
    The First Alphabet Song   23
    Cat Door   24
    In Democritus' Cabin   25
    Digging Up Azaleas Easter Eve   26
    The Place Where a Poem Has Been   27
    Laundry   28
    Picking Penelope Up From
        the True Light Preschool   29
    Saussure, Handy Man   30
    Hey Scarecrow   31
    Driving Past Ostriches   32
    Genetics   33
    Losing Myself In Dishes   34
    Beach   35
    Falling Asleep With Penelope   36
    Finding Myself   37
    Going With Nets   38
    Wanda Vision   39
    Dancing Suite   40
    Dog Moon   41
    Alphabed   42

Down Time   43

     Ice   45
     Still Life With Bathrobe and Cat   46
     Euclid's Happy Hour   47
     Wanda On the Phone With Our Sister-in-Law   48
     Driving Home From the Bumble Bee Pub   49
     What Dreams May Come   50
     Morning At Home With Cat
         and Fifteen-Month-Old   51
     Domestique   52
     Last Call With Belial   53
     Child Development   54
     Winter Break: Composition Primer   55
     Lunch In Brown   56
     Backyard   57
     Teaching Penelope To Ride Her Bike   58
     Working In Movies   59
     High Wire   60
     Morning Is a Castle   61
     Homer's Best Friend   62
     The Geometry Of Commitment   63
     Everyone's a Winner At
         the Six-and-Under Swim Meet   64
     Gifts   65
     Storm   67
     Treasure   68
     Green   69
     Elegy   70
     Imaginative Play (With Spectator)   71
     Hammock   72
     A Momentary Stay   73
     Down Time   74
     The Next Eulogist   75

     About the Author   77

With Gratitude

I would like to thank Limestone College for their generous support in helping this book come to fruition. I would also like to thank all the teachers and poets who have helped in the formation of this book, most notably Angela Ball and DC Berry at the Center for Writers at the University of Southern Mississippi, and also to the outstanding class of poets that I was fortunate to meet and learn from while there.

More personally and more deeply, I would like to thank my children for the beauty and insight they provide me every day and for continuing to teach me about language and its magic. Finally, I would like to thank Farrar, without whom none of this would be possible. Her presence in my life has made all the difference.

Acknowledgements

"Paradise Off Main," *Poetry Motel*, 2003; "A Portrait of Wanda," *Free Lunch*, 2001; "Vacation," *Spillway*, 1999; "Casino Hospital," *Birmingham Poetry Review*, 2006; "Changing Penelope's Diaper," *Barrow Street*, 2001; "Another Reason I Am Not A Painter," *The Southeast Review*, 2003; "Self Portrait," *Iodine*, 2003; "Deciduous," *Cumberland Poetry Review*, 2000; "Cat Door," *Rattle*, 1999; "In Democritus' Cabin," *Free Lunch*, 2004; "Picking Penelope Up from the True Light Preschool," *Cooweescoowee*, 2002; "Saussure, Handy Man," *The Southeast Review*, 2003; "Driving Past Ostriches," *The Southeast Review*, 2003; "Beach," *Red Hawk Review*, 2007; "Falling Asleep with Penelope," *KAKALAK*, 2007; "Going with Nets," *Asheville Poetry Review*, 1995; "Wanda Vision," *LOOP*, 2002; "Dancing Suite," *New Rag Rising*, 2003; "Dog Moon," *Spillway*, 1999; "Ice," *South Carolina Review*, 1999; "Still Life with Bathrobe and Cat," *Snake Nation Review*, 2003; "Wanda on the Phone with our Sister-in-Law," *LOOP*, 2002; "Morning at Home with Cat and Fifteen Month Old," *Rattle*, 2003; "Domestique," *Iodine*, 2003; "Homer's Best Friend," *Main Street Rag*, 2002; "The Geometry of Commitment," *Main Channel Voices*, 2006; "Everyone's a Winner at the Six-and-Under-Swim Meet," *Free Lunch*, 2005; "Gifts," *Spartanburg Journal*, 2006; "Storm," *Illuminations*, 2000; "Green," *Broken Bridge Review*, 2006; "Elegy," *RE:AL*, 2003; "Hammock," *White Pelican Review*, 2004; "Down Time," *Snake Nation Review*, 2003.

"Another Reason I Am Not A Painter," Changing Penelope's Diaper," "A Portrait of Wanda," and "Hammock," *A Millennial Sampler of South Carolina Poetry* (Ninety-Six Press), 2005.

"A Momentary Stay" and "Hammock," *The Southern Poetry Anthology: South Carolina* (Texas Review Press), 2007.

Alphabed

Paradise Off Main

In the beginning, when it's all good,
We nurture ourselves with cigarettes and beer,
Take turns tip-toeing to the kitchen
Between our flights in the futon,
Then out stare the stars, our bodies a parabola,
Limbs interlocking like a cursive *l*
We eat donuts and wrap ourselves in sheets
To topple into the hammock,
Wait for the paper-boy pedaling past,
Wobbling when he reaches for the news,
Then the postman in his wool shorts
And khaki-saucer hat. These are the faces
To witness our proudest devotion,
Our sincerest vows,
Yes and *see you next weekend.*

A Portrait Of Wanda

It's the only one like it,
An eight and a half by eleven reprint
I got especially for the bedside table.
Each night I'm sprawled out in our queen-sized raft
Right between her and the picture of her.

The honeymoon sky goes white as wedding cake,
Sunglasses askew above her porpoise grin,
Shoulder bone laughing forward to stretch black lycra.
Her right hand makes a fist around the stem
Of a martini glass, while pelicans spark
Around her firecracker hair.

I've told you all this without peeking,
Better than the camera. I like it in the middle,
My feet under the covers, combing the sheets
For her pink toes,
And around us, all the water in the world.

Vacation

We rest cross-legged on the silver porch
And talk about ourselves:
Wanda says she has a certain feeling
For our future,
That everything we say we want
Will work its way into our lives.
We fill in the last crosswords together:
Four letters for *Indian garb*,
Seven letters for *Indefinite time*,
And talk some more about what we'll do
Tomorrow or the next day.
Having said everything twice
We look respectfully to the sea
Receding from where we sit
Sipping tea and whiskey,
Reading tide charts and ocean almanacs,
Occasionally lifting our heads
Towards the perfect flight of gulls,
The windy dives of pelicans
Undulating green.

Casino Hospital

The nurses in labor and delivery were laying odds on gender.
They thought it "nice" that we'd waived our right to know.

Under my breath, I asked for the inside track
And they dealt me a Nursing School legend:

*If the heartbeat sounds like a train, it's a boy.
A washing machine, and you have a girl.*

Wanda heard, then rolled her eyes through a hard contraction,
As though I were tossing craps during her hours of reckoning.

I think it's gender confused, I said.
But the nurses had fled, Wanda grimacing as a pit boss.

Later, I found them at their station,
Studying charts like race forms.

I told them if we had a girl, she'd love trains,
If a boy, he'd do the laundry.

I told them that's what Wanda said, and I had to agree.
Still, I anted-up a dime for the underdog.

Changing Penelope's Diaper

Her eyes lock on the blank ceiling
Like she's realized *white*,
Or understands plane geometry.

I spread her legs like a wishbone, peel off the tabs,
Hold her by the ankles with my left hand,
Fold and wrap with my right.

It's then she takes things into her own hands,
Slips one down, then cups it toward her mouth,
Same way Wanda slurps icing off her fingers.

DON'T!
Before I realize she's taught herself a thing
She'll need to know forever.

Another Reason I Am Not a Painter

I keep replaying footage of my body
Free falling into the mulch, a cloudburst of paint descending
Like a bubble in Wanda's lava lamp.
She and I agree I should have been up here
Last summer, straddling the hot tin ladder
With a tray of Latex White, feeling my lips peel in the glare.

When a dragonfly gets lured by the fumes,
I teeter and swat like a hapless King Kong.
The whir of his tiny engine returning, I slide down,
Hook my thumb on a metal rung, slash it
To a cloven hoof. On injured reserve, I take myself inside
To fumble in the drawers for antiseptic, Band-Aids, Chap Stik.

Instead, I fall into a treasure chest
Of Wanda's magical balms, luminous jellies:
Beeswax for eyes, tenderizer for nipples,
Chamomile for long red hair,
My unpainterly blood
Dripping a Chinese alphabet.

Self Portrait

Towel-wrapped in the ice-blue bathroom,

My hair is paper curling in fire.
Shaving foam smears and streaks;
Blood trickles my Adam's apple, my ear.

Water rolls off the end of my pelican's bill.

My eyes are loggerheads
Reading condensation on glass,
Beads clustering into thick fog,

Ready for a finger to write a name.

In a Booth At the House of Pizza, Waiting On the Odysseus Platter

I'm chugging a mug of ice cold Mythos
Gazing out the window at Main:
Streetlights and pedestrians blurry through glass bricks.
Next to that, a steel-framed poster of blue Grecian skies,
Doric columns in the foreground, a simple scape, no people,
And so perfect I know it's a promotional shot,
Know that those drones can't cross the street to Greece,
Can't for anything mount Olympus
And raise their arms triumphantly to Zeus.
I know all this as I wait for my tahini sauce,
Even if I'd missed the name, KITHIRA,
Whitewashed across the heavens, or missed
The fluorescent glare shining where it hangs,
A tad crooked from the sheet rock.

Deciduous

I knew the relationship with Dad had topped out
When he assigned me books he hadn't read himself.
You'll like this one he'd say.
These, too, right up your alley.

He'd joined book clubs (ten for a penny,
No obligation), piled the unbroken spines
Around him like a tiny forest.

Take these, he'd say, tamping a finger
On a stack of titles. I'd lean back,
Thumbing through the smells of literature,
While he folded the crossword in his lap.

Then he'd walk to the park,
Fling birdseed the way a sprinkler
Tosses water. Pigeons grubbed
Around his feet, and he clucked awhile
Before churning back home to watch movies.

Back at my rented duplex,
I'd scatter the books like jigsaw pieces,
Try to make sense of the picture.

Nightshape

In the perfect moment
Before sleep, a cat
Lights on my back, kneads the space
Between my shoulder blades
And curls into a steady purr,
An old clock winding down.
Wanda's asleep, shape of an s,
The bowl of her bottom
Cupped in my palm.
The dog bends to his arrhythmic licking,
As I creep toward tomorrow's dream,
When I'll jerk from a fetal position,
Clear the dough from my throat,
And stretch into an arrow.
Everyone's feet on the floor.

The First Alphabet Song

A B C D G F G
H R J K yellow pea.
Who's R yes yellow pea
Who's R yes yellow in a pea
Nest time won't you yellow in a pea.
Who's R yes E-OO V
Double OO X Y and Z.
How you know my number Z,
Nest time nest time nest time me.

Cat Door

Belly brought a pigeon through
In the dark morning;
I could hardly scold him;
He was so proud, even righteous,
With his platter eyes, tense jaws
Snug around the limp neck,
The shut wings.
I rolled over, hoped it was a dream,
Hoped the intermittent flapping wasn't real,
Or at least that it would end.
When I got up for coffee
And returned to bed for the news
I saw it clearly:
Unpunctured and perfect,
Bloodless above my pillow,
The gift I never deserve.

In Democritus' Cabin

Found a house with no roof; just a well,
Made it our fort, aimed pellet guns at glass,
At beer cans, old shoes and crutches.
We made up a history for that house:
A toothless old man surrounded by hounds and kudzu.

And once when peering down
Into the echoing hole, we saw him
Rise through wet, black leaves
To pull us down. We yelped
Like our own dogs that beat us home.

Digging Up Azaleas Easter Eve

Wanda rigged a beaming flashlight, coal-miner style, to my hard hat.
I was the moon to every overworked worm in town,
A big dumb ass with one cartoon idea swaying
Between a shovel, a garden hose and Jose Cuervo.
Next door, Ms. Begonia served umbrella drinks,
Asked if I planned on digging all night,
Checking her wrist the way carpenters do at quitting time.
I assured her I was in it for the long haul,
Wouldn't rest till every azalea stump was heaped
On the curb as one muddy creature.
For three hours Wanda and Ms. Begonia chatted politics –
The state, the body, the orgasm – in whispers.
I loosened the maze of roots with each thrust,
Stabbing through sinews of burlap,
Piling up cool mounds of different-colored dirt
Till at once, I noticed them noticing me,
As if I'd sprouted from that same loam
Just to dig my own body back to hell.

The Place Where a Poem Has Been

Driving on in the morning frost
I see deer among cattle,
Steam emanating from their flanks,
All heads lifting in more than usual harmony.
Further down, a field of blackbirds,
And a new way of seeing spots of ink
Spilt on a white page.
The snow man stands
Precisely where the farm children rolled him,
His accoutrements pieced together
From all their parents' closets.
And behind everything, the white smoke
From the factory
Drifting into the still whiter sky.

Laundry

Takes the best seat in the house,
Spills over the edges like poured champagne,
Settles into puddles of panties and stockings;
A red-light sculpture in repose.

I'm hunched over, walking with a warm mommy load
Clutched in my arms,
A Loony Toon turtle toting his own shell.

Once the chair's re-upholstered in aromatic cotton,
I parachute a king-sized sheet over the wrinkled pile,
A homemade pillow to hide in
When the family wagon rolls home.

That's me with the screwy grin, burrowed
Deep in all our clothes, which I intend to fold
When the audience arrives, calling out my name.

Picking Penelope Up From the True Light Preschool

My Mercury's stuck in a phalanx of Troopers and Suburbans,
The day's crossword complete, flapped open in the passenger side.
Everyone inches toward the orange cones,
Ms. Weathersby loading the kids
With their daily words.

Penelope beams in the high noon,
Climbs in the car with a candy cane.
It's a J, she says, *for Jesus*,
Ms. Weathersby grinning, mouth curled into a manger.
P says the red's for blood, the white for *purty*.
Purty? I repeat, who's purty?

The baby Jesus, silly,
Laughing like a three-foot Santa while I strap her in
And punch us down the road. Around the corner,
I tell her candy canes aren't for Jesus,
They're for children, but you don't have to tell Weathersby.

Some people find the Lord everywhere, I say--
Life's one great big Golgotha,
A puzzle spelling redemption
In crisscrossed letters.
By the time I'm done, Penelope's asleep.

At the curb beside our home,
I remember myself at four,
In the back seat, being talked at,
How tiring to pump myself in the swing,
How exhausting, communion.

Saussure, Handy Man

Ferdinand whittles a new pencil point,
Marks a crow's foot and saws the wood,
Smooth as shellac. He's adding a wing
To the parlor he added last week,
The pencil soaring through the space between his ear
And the two by four.

He's just starting, a team of inspectors
On the way with levels and tape measures.
Ferdy has a reputation for cutting corners,
Fudging blue prints, forgetting joists and dormers.

They pencil their comments —always the same:
An A+ for craftsmanship, but no one knows
What he had in mind.
He explains to the officials,
It's the unfinished product we really desire;
Anything we build must lack integrity.

Hey Scarecrow

I put my foot in the road,
Walk the field no one owns
To chat up the scarecrow,
Cross-hairs on the night sky.
I drink a Blue Ribbon
And move the stars
By blinking one eye,
Then the other.

Leaning down on the grain,
I fit the straw man in Orion's belt.
What kind of brain makes a man
Leave home
Only to have the stars
Shoot him back?

Driving Past Ostriches

Is like watching my whole morning
Flash before my eyes, the way Wanda pulls me
On top, eases me awake and out of the cold.

They stoop in the fog, making the beast
With four wings, or a two-headed snowman
Washed gray.

They rise and wiggle out of the mist,
Blurry through the windshield
Reflecting brief light on their prehistoric bodies.

Genetics

I was born at the beginning of happy hour,
A fact never lost on Dad.
For years, 4 o'clock was the neon hour
For popping bourbon,
His daily commitment to happy birthdays.

My own son was born during cartoons,
Wanda's veins coursing with Stadol.
You'll feel a little drunk the doctor said.
I sat on the vinyl daybed, brow on fist,
All green and thin,
Like Popeye before spinach.

They released me after the photos, the tale of the tape.
Mama needs rest they said,
And you could use a shower, maybe a nap.
I followed the color-coded arrows out, then the streetlights
To the "Music City Diner."

It's nothing like happy hour, now.
Still, I take a beer with the Yosemite Sam Omelet.
It could be anytime, anyplace.
Hell, my dad might do-si-do through the swinging doors,
Like Foghorn Leghorn proclaiming the hour,
Never one to miss a birthday, or an opportunity.

Losing Myself In Dishes

My fingers make each plate squeak.
Then I catch a glimpse of shocked hair,
My silhouette (a cartoon Commemorative
Bearing my Presidential mug shot,
Austerely smug and suitable
For drawing rooms or scrapbooks)
Slanted momentarily in fluorescence.
When the last suds circle the drain,
My only reflection poses in the window pane,
The ceiling light a blank thought-bubble
Set to pop in the dark.

Beach

I have two bare feet
To negotiate the boardwalk,
Strewn with downed limbs,
In the tow of an aged spaniel
In quick pursuit of a sandpiper.

With how glad an eye
I take inventory on the ocean,
The nearby folding chairs,
The high travel of clouds, the sun
Inching along its perfect arc.

All phyla of shells and smoothed relics
Gather in pools near the groin.
Human forms, as well,
Fleshy as they stroll slowly into breakers:
The pelican formations up, the porpoise spume out

And the book I brought along for show.

Falling Asleep With Penelope

Once she's named everything in her room
And murdered the ABC song,
She scrambles into bed and pecks me *night night*.
I become the birdman of her bedroom,
Waiting to fly the coop, peeking through eye-slits
At her baboon eyes, her goofy grin
Watching me watching her not falling asleep.

I fake a low-snore, zzzzz, and she fakes
A laugh, says I'm a kookydaddy and reaches for a book.
I'm asleep I hum, remembering to resume
Unconscious breathing, slow as static.
I lead by example, and when I awake,
Her sleepy feet are nestled in my shirt,
Her dead arms hooking me in a headlock.

Getting out of the rack,
I assemble myself one big piece at a time,
A jigsaw puzzle for beginners.
Down the hall, I slip into bed
Beside the life-sized version
Curling my body next to hers,
Nudging the cats into their own soft landings.

Finding Myself

I never went in for totem animals,
Let my daily feats of domestic facility pass
Without giving them a tail.

This morning, though, my footfalls didn't creak the floor
When I sprawled on the shag and reached toward a spot of sun.
At dinnertime, I stalked Wanda, lovingly, through the kitchen.
And late at night, I awoke on top of the sheets,
Snuggling a pillow.

And just now when I stretched out of bed
And slinked into the living room,
Nobody turned a head.

Going With Nets

Down along a petrified dock of wood
We carry cast nets and icy bourbon.
Bare-foot with trousers rolled jaggedly to our shins
And mosquitoes angling around our tracks,
Four feet follow a curve where water
Wets the sand foamy and white
Till we reach an adequate spot for launching wide nets.
The first toss is merely for practice,
A way of easing into it, and the three or four minnows
It nets are not kept.
Then over and over, improving routinely:
Swaying our bodies to the sea-rhythm,
Dangling the girth of nets from our strangely strong hands,
Tasting the salty, weighted rope-ends clutched in our teeth,
Released when the rhythm is just so, and our nets catch air,
Circle seaward, hit water and disappear in dark green
Between us and them. Then holding the rope
We gauge its slow descent, its single thud on the bottom.
One yank skyward brings them to us:
Shrimp and silvery minnows
Pulled from cool quickness into judgment's light.

Wanda Vision

In an effort to avoid transparency,
I nixed the Valentine Negligée.
Instead, kicked my dust into Mercury's Shoe Cellar,
All the way back to the neon slippers.
Though many seemed to whisper
Orthopedic, I handled the open boxes,
Fondled the suede and corduroy,
The terri-cloth and satin.
I couldn't help myself, settled on a pair
Of furry blues, little Cookie Monsters
Without eyes. Luxurious nests for her glittering toes,
Her voluptuous arches
Springing into bed, legs
Like two boomerangs bringing me home.

Dancing Suite

I've moved a rocking chair into the bathroom
So when Penelope takes five from her dance recital,
I'll have someplace to sit. She twists her body on the pot
Like a quarter ride at the grocery, then clutches the sides smiling.
Sit there daddy. Close door daddy.

I flip the Cosmo ads, older beauties, lanky-necked as giraffes,
Till she hands me Kermit's book
On the proper procedures and techniques for successful, stress-free evacuation.
The key, Kermit says, is to understand it's a process.
Just relax, I say, it'll come.

I sit in my corner like a dog
Who's learned to beg from a distance;
My eyebrows rise when I hear the deliberate sprinkle,
The emphatic plop. She dips her head between her knees,
Look daddy, it just come out my body.

I hold her hand through the rest: wiping, flushing.
It's the coda of swirling water
That sends her chirping through the house,
I'm the nakey jaybird.

Dog Moon

Wanda and I start with the wind behind us,
Walk till the sun's a smear, staying close
To the shore-line, where half is sky and half is sea.
In wet-hard sand our footsteps
Follow like hyphens past sea-oats and crab-holes.

Our dog runs loose,
Hurdles ahead of the tide's length
The way a pelican glides above breaking surf.
She disappears into dunes, noses everything,
Brow-wrinkled, body-still, then lunges,
Laughing in all directions, turns and slides,
Re-strides and splashes,
Shakes the ocean from her body.

We march along in straight lines,
Bowing our heads into a breeze,
Eyes on the tract before us,
A new sliver of moon
Balanced above our roof.

Alphabed

Wanda always says *Home is where the groin sleeps*,
And most nights we're two bags of sand,
An A-frame reading in the dark, or a sweet-lovely *I*
Surrounded by flopped off sheets.

Some nights when the moon glows in
From down the hall, our daughter heaves herself
From bed, waddles the hardwood floor
And presses the cracked door wide,

Scales my torso and the swell of pillows
To drop like a docked fish,
Nuzzling her face into mom's back,
Pointing her toes to hook my ribs.

We lie like a cursive *H* under the steady fan
Till sonny boy climbs from his crib
And pulls his body aboard:
A crew on a mission for the sun,

Or a single hunk of driftwood
Misshapen in the moonlit room.

Down Time

Ice

It used to excite me to see
The wear on statues, see spring
As the ever-fresh idiot
Getting its feet burnt off
In a late frost, the statue
Just putting on another coat of soot.

Today I look out a window
At the sunlight and shade,
Follow the breezy shadow-line and look away.
Three seconds all told: concrete and dirt.

I cheer up when I move
To the kitchen for a drink,
And someone else
Has emptied the ice cubes
Into the box and filled the trays
With water.

Still Life With Bathrobe and Cat

Standing in my bathrobe like a rundown Marcel Marceau,
I wave Wanda and the kiddies down the street.

When I lounge in the easy chair with a poem,
The cat makes her silent leap, flares her tail in my face,
And settles her primitive hydraulics onto the page.

Her purr plays the lead to the continuo of the house,
The treble of birds joining in with the drone of crickets.

I'd planned on using my pen as a dart,
Aiming for the bull's eye of a sleepy image.

Instead, I trace the feline outline that's already there.
She responds with a riff, tail gently whipping
Till she's stretched into a new form.
I'll trace that one, too.

Pretty soon, it resembles a Nude Descending a Staircase,
My happy accident, easy contours filling the page,
Day's work done, cat curled up now,
Just in time for the *Early Bird Matinee*.

Euclid's Happy Hour

I was planning only on a martini,
The baby taking a nap,

So nearly gone, the last sips
Of milk gurgled from his mouth
Until the motion of swinging stuck
In his lullaby, re-played
Like a scratched record and popped him
From the drowsy rocker like a small flame,
Whispering *'ing . . . 'ing*, pointing out the window,
Nodding his head like grandpa near the end.

It's night-night time I'd said.
We need a nap now so we can swing later.
No no, 'ing now, arms bouncing as if to fly,
As if my talking had twirled him to the door:
Open dis . . . open dis.

So here I am, pushing a plastic swing
Weeeeeee
His head still nodding, knees pure in sunlight,
Push . . . mo-uh,
As if progressing towards a circle.

Wanda On the Phone With Our Sister-In-Law

I'm feigning sleep, the ageless pose:
A *Parents'* magazine flopped open across my chest,
Like bird wings in the background of a painting.

Craning, I can just make out the voice in the phone,
No words, but a tone of distrust,
Like a voice screaming under water.

Wanda blurts clear across town,
Like I always say,
You make your own bed,
Then sleep on the sofa.

Jarred, I check for droolage while the questions
Circulate my limbo. I'm the one asleep on the sofa, aren't I?
Did I bozo? I mean, I know the latest on pull-up diapers at naptime,
But have I been dreaming?

My brother at the *Bumble Bee Pub* knows all.
He'll be sitting there in the time-out corner
Waiting for my frame to brighten the door,
And wouldn't a snort of tequila clear my mind?

I shoot Wanda the fly-sign, jingle the keys out the door.
She pinches the phone between her shoulder and ear,
Head cocked like our dog's, confused or piqued.

Driving Home from the Bumble Bee Pub

The Mercury buzzes, its front seat a sofa,
Speedometer staring me down like a clock face at the therapist's office,
Steering wheel loose enough to twirl with a single paw.

For now, though, I observe proper safety procedures:
Hands at two and ten, seat belt clicked,
Eyes on the dotted line.

Windows down, wind flings the smoke from my hair.
Every pot-hole reassures me that home is a place
Where I'm driven by heart.

I flip the radio full blast;
It mimics the bar-room feedback
Still ringing my ears.

Leaning against the wheel,
I glance at the stars, paint the straight lines in between:
My own constellation,

Great Wanda Panda,
Blinking above home.

What Dreams May Come

Three weeks after I'd dragged an Igloo of shrimp and champagne
Down maternity row, Wanda was back spinning cocktails,
Leaving me with the ten pounds of flesh to pamper.

A dozen years ago I had my liquored up fantasies,
Fixed on Kitty's barmaid hands,
Her comfortable jeans, or the inevitable slit
In her skirt. She said happy hour lasted
Till I left and fetched bourbon,
Her ears and everything bending to the bar.

Now I'm home, doubled up on diapers,
Mac whimpering into a snore while Penelope renders
The Unabridged Tales of Peter Rabbit.

Wanda's still trotting between tables,
Bringing home stacks of crumpled bills
For our Christmas fund. I know their bar-fly eyes
Better than my own, ebbing to the bottom
Of the glass, returning to her blowsy march,
Bringing neat remedies with her white white hands.

We've called it a day in the children's bedroom,
The moon wedging through the window,
Dragging its slow beam across the floor.

Morning At Home With Cat and Fifteen-Month-Old

Belly's in the alley, hunched over, chewing.
A lizard mouth gapes on gravel,
Just the mouth, an organ sac,
And a tail swaying like a broken metronome.

I change my son's diaper;
He lies back, jawing, reaching for anything,
Writhing on carpet.

The cat door flaps open and shut;
Sonny boy chants *Beh-lee . . . Beh-lee*,
Who drops a new lizard in the corner
And jabs it there like Muhammad Ali measuring the knockout.

Sonny boy claps faster, inhales laughter,
Shrieks *BEH-LEE*
Clinching his fists overhead as the victor.

I stop the fight, tote the loser out on a paper towel,
And flatten it with a brick, Belly stalking me now.

My son waddles to the cat door, pushes it open,
Calling *'old yoo, 'old yoo,*
His arms outstretched like Frankenstein's.

Domestique

I'm barefoot, juggling avocados in the kitchen,
My son dribbling Lucky Charms,
Cheering, *trya egg daddy-o*.

My face goes flat as Buster Keaton's,
And I chicken leg-it to the fridge,
Drop my rag to select a large Free Range,
And add it to the Aerial Cooking Show:

I give them a twirl, the little mono-hipped egg
And crowned avocados thudding my palms
To tips to air, me counting--
Ten catches per spoonful, till he screams *all gone!*

I take my bow as avocados bounce and the egg falls
Through dust-mote spotlights, rolls uncracked
Behind the hutch, a small miracle,
Sonny boy oozing Technicolor, his mouth filled with stars.

Last Call With Belial

Alright Milton, I know you're a Puritan,
But even that allows you an appreciation
For the duties and pleasures of euphemism.
Let's just crack the body's Newgate for one night,
Ease down to *Adam's Pub*, knock back a few
And ogle the barmaids, offer our seats
To a couple of Jezebels and lather them in Sir John Suckling.
Do you think, with a little encouragement, you could
Get up and jig a gypsy, or watusi
As the Godfather of Soul?
It'll feel good to cut loose and please the mob.
Tomorrow, the sun will still inch past the clouds,
Slither through the cracks of your cottage
And tap your forehead like Michael's sword.
But for now, the old moon's still smiling,
And I know a place where the door flaps all night.

Child Development

Universal sounds, marathon drooling.
Rolling and rocking. Knee walking.

Feet first everywhere,
His fluff of white hair a tiny mouse

Running into walls. Biting. Hiding.
Holding himself with both hands.

Dismantling towers and castles.
Demolishing small equipment.

Laughing appropriately.
Sleeping through things.

Winter Break: Composition Primer

It's my daughter gets me back in the swing,
Twisting my arm into the chair beside hers,
A snowman accumulating on her cardboard canvas.
I'm a giant elf in training,
Till she says, *draw a dada house.*

I begin with a garden,
Aiming for immaculate hedgerows
And corn high as my head,
Sketch myself, instead, into an uneven field
Ravaged by deer and buzzards.

I nail the scarecrow, though,
While she rat-a-tat-tats a white crayon,
Flecking snow around a thick man,
Brown sticks for arms,
Red scarf, black smile.

I scoot to my knees,
Nosing over the tic-tac-toe roofing,
The Caligari chimney and its squiggles of smoke.
Before I can tone up the split-rail fence,
She pushes her portrait aside and shoulders the door,
Runs headlong into the clouds of her own breath
In the bright and visible air.

Lunch In Brown

High noon on free Friday, so coast to the museum,
Stroll through Klee's twittering machines;
Toothpick limbs, fragile ovals, birdy countenance
Against layers of industrial brown.

Outside, I doctor a corndog with relish and mustard,
Eat it all steaming on the corner,
Keep truckin' with the blended sauces
Crusting the corners of my mouth.

At the *Corner Pocket* I jig some bourbon,
And circle the table behind the 8 ball,
Crack each shot two, three, even four rails,
The cue just making the rounds, dodging every color.

I lean in again and again,
The stick lined up beneath my nose,
Legs forming an isosceles triangle with the ground.
Scuffed loafers slick as wheels.

Backyard

Sonny boy's a little Buddha
Waiting for me to click
The swing's harness around his eternal torso,
Let him fly.

I back away, clench the wormwood handle
Of a shovel, and announce my game,
I'm gonna scoop that poo.

He dangles silently,
Then, slowing, laughs in a lurch,
Legs flapping like hoses overfilled with water.

I catapult several days' worth
Through the air, the dogs
Running their circles, then stake the shovel,

Pull his carriage eye-level,
And let it drop, its perfect arc returning,
The shovel our totem
Rising from invisible roots.

Teaching Penelope To Ride Her Bike

I learn to run like a goose,
Bent, accelerating,
Holding the banana seat
While she serpentines over wet leaves,
Her arms noodle-dancing with the handlebars.
I cool my flight feathers, legs gearing down,
Eyes ripening into large brown eggs.
Her back steadies, wheels straighten.
I'm stiller than a floating decoy,
Penelope whizzing past the Dead End sign
Without instructions for turning.

Working In Movies

When I strut up the street alone with Art Blakey
Moanin' in my ears, I know I am the director of my life
As a feature length. I watch red turn green and ramble
Across the white diagonals down Pendleton Street,
Where I'll duck in for a pint and have whatever's special,
The infectious alto sax ushering me to my favorite table
Near the bar, where I order and wait and dream of being edited.
From here, my direction is limited: the waitress a born improviser,
The kitchen staff on their own clock.
I cannot know who'll stroll in and join me or not;
I can only anticipate the next solo
As the band plays along discretely
During this slow-moving comedy-drama.
She brings another black and tan like a scented demotion,
From director to musical advisor,
Banking on the 5 Spot be-bop to remind me I'm here.
By the time I've settled up with the world's next great actress
And headed for home, I'm all the way down the chain
Of command to key grip, pressing myself inside,
The children, skit-ready, leaping at me
With their highs and lows, their own scripts to sell.
I grin and try to join the fun by crawling on all fours
In the carpeted, lamp-lit den, a new stunt-double,
Giving a well-earned rest to the family dog,
Who shuffles back to her trailer for the night,
Just as my cameo comes on, right before bedtime,
Where all tomorrow's stories come true.

High Wire

People say I should hang up my slippers,
Quit while I'm still in clover.
But they love crossing their fingers,
Holding their breath while I toe the platform.

Maybe I got into this business
For a red cape, or maybe to see my name
Behind an impressive list of hyphenated adjectives.
Or was it simply a dare?

No matter, I'm swaying up here again,
Two-stepping the tight-rope,
All my energies to the balls of my feet,
Focused as a yogi, adding depth to the sky.

Morning Is a Castle

A thousand miles away,
Across a mote of brown carpet,

A fort of pillows with a ceiling
Of sagging blankets.

My children's feet stretch out of windows
Like limber watchmen from a turret.

Inside, they grip flashlights,
Dim beams darting along the walls.

Around their little dream of a campfire,
They speak in tiny giggles.

I lean in, straining my ears for any word
To take as invitation.

Homer's Best Friend

Before he became a poet, Homer had a dog.
Not a seeing-eye-dog.
They walked into town, all the merchants
Wondering if Homer knew there was a cur on his tail.
He drank until he could almost see,
Then navigated the fields of Elysium,
The dog keeping pace.
Homer curled up and groaned under the stars.
Deep into REM, his body twitched like a fallen soldier's.
The dog licked loose hexameters into his ear,
A long, damp tongue dactylic on his dizzy head.

The Geometry Of Commitment

By the time the clock's big hand had nearly circled
The small hand, the therapist had given us the goods;
Marriage is not a 50/50 proposition;
The best you can hope for is 100% half the time.
My brow furrowed like an obedient spaniel's.
He whistled on, *meaning you get what you want*
Half the time; the other half you don't.

I should've known better,
But I felt after an hour I could try:
Yes, I blabbed, it's like parallel play;
You each do your own thing,
Sharing blocks to build separate mazes.

His smile sent me to kindergarten,
As he removed his horned-rims and squeezed
Wanda's knee. *No, there are no straight lines,*
Not in nature or in marriage, no straight lines
Anywhere. On the wall, the big hand
Began a victory lap while I leaned back,
Stretching my legs on the square rug.

Everyone's a Winner At the Six-and-Under Swim Meet

You know the stroke, what's it called?
When the body splashes from one end
To the other without drowning,

A fish before fins,
A little fetal wriggling
Unraveling into a dogpaddle.

There's no beat or stable pace, nothing to name it by,
A kind of survival of the non fittest,
Passing from the shallow end to the deep.

A frog with no legs.
Paralysis in motion,
As if the will is all that can move us.

Gifts

I tried joking at first,
That this one would solidify her bust
In the Mother-in-Law Hall of Fame.
Not one, or even two, but four ducks
Huddled in an Easter basket, shivering
Right under my kids' noses.
Two were mallards, nearly ready to fly,
The others yellow, but would morph
Into sitting ducks, white and fat.
It was quick, the exchange, and later,
The ducks' development. I remain
Convinced that someone fed them plutonium
While we were away.
How else to explain their mercurial growth,
Their impressive and emerging stench,
Their complete need for hours of dotage?
And still they were neglected.
My kids, who swore they would not,
Lost interest, and I with the dogs,
Embraced my neglect with bitter zeal.
I guess that is why
Lately I have noticed birds diving
At my windshield when I leave home.
And yesterday, while I folded laundry
In neat little rows, a sparrow torpedoed
Into the glass where I stood.
My wife told her mother it was beginning to cause
Marital strife, and suddenly, I started to grow as well,
Not real growth, not like the ducks,
But growth nonetheless,
In my mother-in-law's imagination:
I became the non-nurturer of my own brood.
She promised she had a better home
Lined up, and chuckled that we'd kept them

Continued

As long as we had.
I hadn't known there were options,
Just as I hadn't known last Christmas
That I would begin prematurely to lose my hearing
When Santa stuffed a drum kit down our chimney.

Storm

The air lulls.
The sky turns a color
Only it may become

And turns again sooner than
We can place it.
Strangeness in my skin

And deeper. Outdoors bursts
Into beads to keep itself
From drowning.

All this from a front porch:
The drift of sky, dazzle of rain.
We learn again to breathe water.

Treasure

My son, shirtless and barefooted, emerged
From hours of piracy with a confession.
I don't want to keep secrets from my family,
So, Dad, close your eyes
And he revealed within his small hand
My pocket knife, lost for weeks,
A simple, sharp blade, retractable.
All I could muster was 'Thanks!
I've been missing that,' the terrible irony
Of my parents' divorce in mind,
Those family secrets.
He led me to the place he'd found it,
His own imaginary 'X,' the drawer from my bedside table,
Toted away into a corner of his playroom,
Filled with all my booty:
The things on my list not yet scratched through,
The things to look for when I got home,
A buckeye, handkerchief, wedding band,
My copy of *The Odyssey*, which I needed for class,
Well-read and coming off its binding,
Like something knocking around
The bottom of the ocean a very long time.

Green

At the pool, late summer, Sunday night
Closing in on closing time,
Most of the kids already done
To homework and packed lunches.

Tans fade even as the sun
Dips into the treeline.
Whistles from the high school field
Ring out behind me.

Tree frogs warble and buzzards circle the woods,
Kudzu vines amok and everyone with barefeet
Knows that nothing lasts,
That nothing dies for long.

Elegy

When I was five I watched the orange jumpsuits
Back-hoe the ground and push the dirt,
Drop a burlapped tree
Into a hollow
Between the road and the new walk:
A morning's splash of cement in cleared space.
I learned to measure my walks
By frames of concrete:
Gumwads, ant-hills, slopes and cracks
Where tree roots knuckled up pavement.
Weeds parted the smog
Of cars and trucks filing from town,
The sidewalk splitting like the sloppy wake
Of a slow-moving ship.

Imaginative Play (With Spectator)

I know I am predisposed to cry
GENIUS! Anytime one of my little auteurs
Invents a game or cliché.

But when sonny boy bangs out a tune
On the out-of-tune piano the previous owners left
Outside at the new house,

Well, I applaud my own resourcefulness
For having rolled it back inside
And wiped it down with a damp cloth

So he can sit there in complete control
Of his right hand, representing the damsel,
And his left, the rough beast

Bonging and sloughing
Toward the center of the keyboard,
The damsel ambling easily along

Into the grasping teeth of the left hand, just as I'd imagined,
A mess of euphonious fingers.
What else to do but clap?

Clap for me because I am Dad,
Come here to say matter-of-factly
That I have never seen such a production

Of the little girl and the big bad whatshisname.
So bravo. BRAVO! I sing,
Sit straight and attentive

To see how those little fingers
Will elude the other half of invention
And make it home safely once again.

Hammock

I back into it like an early moon,
Each muscle lapsing into perfect atrophy;
My only way of flying, a low-country trick on physics.

Above me, wrens nest in the abandoned light fixture
Hanging from the tongue and groove,
Their flight from under the porch's eave

Like the jetstream on channel 8.
I'm a lazy weatherman who's traded afternoon showers
For the intricate cartography of wings.

Better than the sky is how I put it
To Mr. Windchime next door, his science
For reading weather: bamboo, porcelain, pewter

All hewn into spears, stars, pelicans
Twinkling and flapping an uneven song.
I'm slowing down,

A stationary droplet suspended in the roped parallelograms,
Not even that, no rain in sight,
A guy held up by holes, by nothing, same as constellations.

A Momentary Stay

It's an unusually lazy stretch of afternoon,
In-laws out, children hiking the well-worn holiday trails
With Mom this 5th of July.

And I with the dogs listless on the dock,
The lake water rolling up,
Sopping the green banks.

I'm Hamlet in a damp bathing suit.
Read or write? Another beer? Spot of rum?
A mixed hound noses a tennis ball at my feet.

I sip and listen
For the tires returning
On the gravel drive.

That's when the thing happens that makes me think
I'm the guy in a Frost poem –
A thick bird swerving through low branches

And out of sight. I think he must have seen me
So idle with a book and a pad before me,
Must've, by God, decided he'd make up my mind,

And do so in such a blackish blur
That I couldn't name him, couldn't,
Like a 5-year-old boy with Audubon in his pocket,

Say *Hawk* or *Crow* or *Turkey*,
Could only reach for the pad and leave
The mysteries of literature for another hour.

This much I can scribble, up to the moment
Where the thing vanishes,
Just as it had appeared.

Down Time

Wanda bought a computer desk on the way home.
Close-out. Assembly required.
I'm on home detail, unshaven for days, t-shirt and boxers,
Feet tough as sandpaper from scuffing paths between appliances.

Me and the kiddies are a machine,
Oiled and whirling, hitting all the buttons:
Froot Loops, a stroll to the park, poo-shovelling before lunch –
Ketchup and macaroni – then *the Cat of many countries* and siesta.

While they're off in Nod, I separate the 178 pieces,
Line up the panels, marry rear tube A to rear tube AA,
Fasten the L clips with the silver 9/16th metal screws,
Secure panels E, F, and G with the 5/8th wood screws,
Pop in the front tubes and couple the end plugs.

After an hour I'm banging around like an old lawn mower.
Wanda wades in and hovers like an incompetent magician's angel.
I snatch the beer she holds out and re-load the electric screwdriver,
Get shaking on the retractable keyboard tray.

I'm down to 64 screws and up to three beers,
Wanda and the gang sucking on popsicles.
When I'm done at 4:45, she hands me the children like a paycheck,
Says *don't forget to water* and drifts off to bubble bath,
Loufahs herself for ladies' night at the *Honeydew Tavern*.

I take the front porch, like I've conquered the world,
Flick long arcs from the hose. I've got a well-disguised jump on happy hour,
The desk complete, 11 screws left, a new outfit warming in the dryer.
I scratch my tummy while the children shuck and jive their suburban rain dance,
Calling down the city water in deliberate sheets.

The Next Eulogist

Let me begin by expressing my very deep,
Very sincere gratitude to the family
For selecting me among hundreds
To be one of a dozen or so to speak here today.

I hope only to render unto Caesar that which is Caesar's
Within my allotted time before bestowing the floor
To our next honoree.
If I should glance at my wrist,
Please don't take it wrong;
I have no place better to be,
But merely want to keep our program on pace,
Or at least as on pace as we were
When I began to address our dearly departed.

I have my memories, as we all have,
And I see no point in projecting mine,
Rife though they are,
Onto your mourning psyches.
But rather, a moment of quiet reflection
Will allow us all to ponder our own images,
Our own compilations of greatest hits
Along with which we may hum
And in which we may revel
From this day forward,
For it was a life, indeed, filled with great hits.

The English essayist, William Hazlitt,
Said some remarkable and poignant things
For such an occasion, and who can forget
Emerson's definition of success?

But my inner clock tells me
That we are ready for the baton to be passed,
For the page to be turned,

For someone else to claim the stage
And keep this little record
Of our great friend spinning,
As there are so many others
That have something to say.

About the Author

Alex Richardson's poetry has appeared in such places as *Free Lunch*, *Barrow Street*, *Birmingham Poetry Review*, *The Southeast Review*, *Snake Nation Review* and *The Southern Poetry Anthology*. He is Chair of the English Department at Limestone College where he teaches Creative Writing, Film History, Modern Poetry and Shakespeare. He lives in Spartanburg, South Carolina with his wife and two children.

www.ingramcontent.com/pod-product-compliance
Lightning Source LLC
Chambersburg PA
CBHW071030080526
44587CB00015B/2566